333 WORD BOOK™
WORLD at WORK

Illustrated by Robert Durham

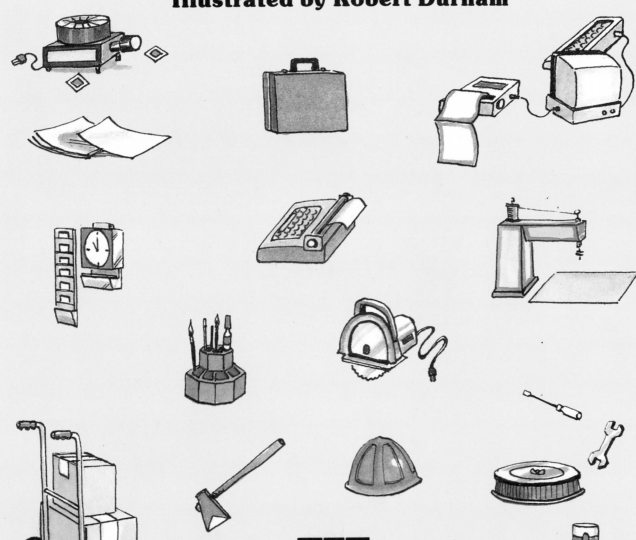

CLB

Colour Library Books

IN A TOY FACTORY

 lunch box

 timecards

 doll's house

 toy duck

time clock

pressure gauge

safety helmet

welder

torch

stapler

robot

vacuum cleaner

scissors

packing material

awl

teddy bear

fork-lift

sprinkler

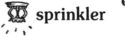

extension lead

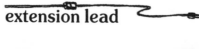

football

exit sign

toy lorry

jack-in-the-box

thread

ing machine

coffee machine

fan

polystyrene cups

fluorescent light

service lift

compressor

spray gun

apron

grease gun

building bricks

rocking horse

supervisor

clipboard

conveyor belt

cart

fridge

AT A GARAGE

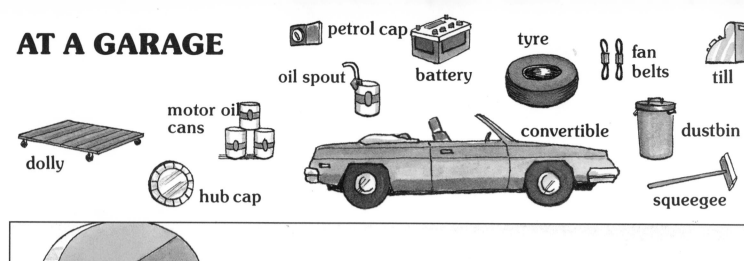

petrol cap

oil spout

battery

tyre

fan belts

till

motor oil cans

dolly

convertible

dustbin

hub cap

squeegee

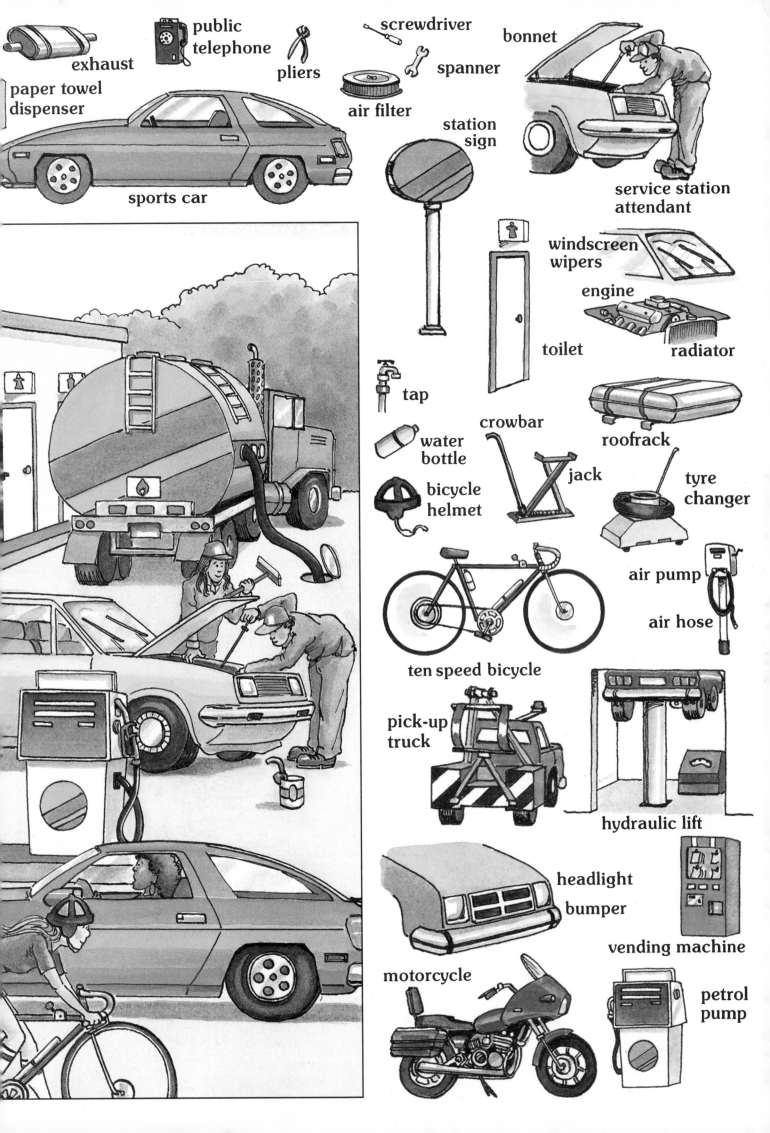

exhaust

paper towel dispenser

public telephone

pliers

screwdriver

spanner

air filter

bonnet

sports car

station sign

service station attendant

windscreen wipers

engine

tap

toilet

radiator

water bottle

crowbar

roofrack

bicycle helmet

jack

tyre changer

air pump

air hose

ten speed bicycle

pick-up truck

hydraulic lift

headlight

bumper

vending machine

motorcycle

petrol pump

AT THE AIRPORT

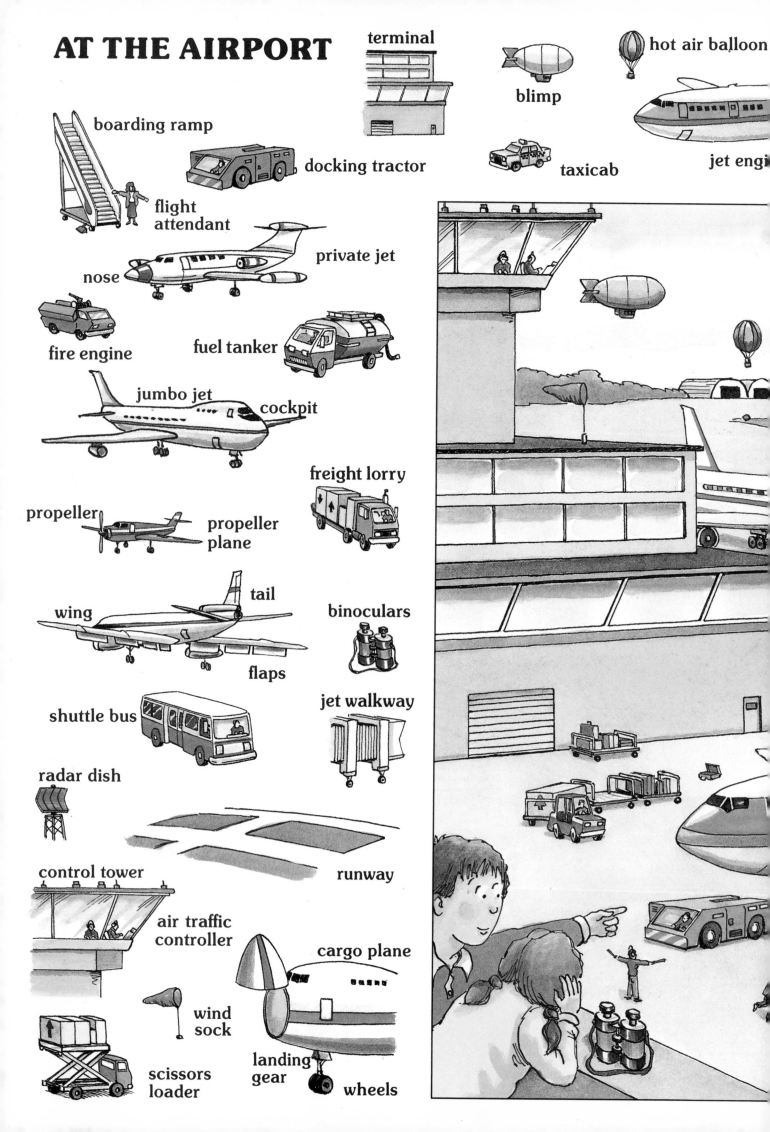

terminal

hot air balloon

blimp

boarding ramp

docking tractor

taxicab

jet engine

flight attendant

nose

private jet

fire engine

fuel tanker

jumbo jet

cockpit

freight lorry

propeller

propeller plane

wing

tail

binoculars

flaps

shuttle bus

jet walkway

radar dish

control tower

runway

air traffic controller

cargo plane

wind sock

scissors loader

landing gear

wheels

jetliner rudder

rotors

helicopter

docking director

luggage trolley

passenger

ambulance landing pad

generator hangars

ON THE RAILWAY

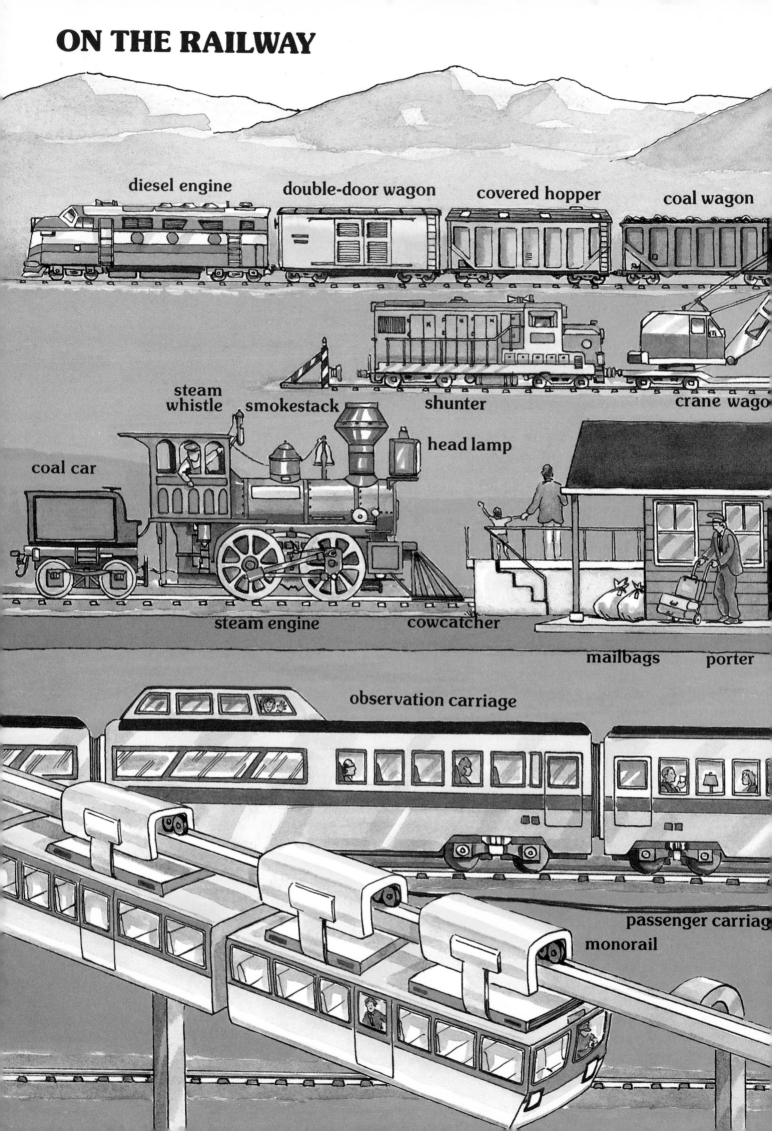

diesel engine

double-door wagon

covered hopper

coal wagon

shunter

crane wago

steam whistle

smokestack

head lamp

coal car

steam engine

cowcatcher

mailbags

porter

observation carriage

passenger carriag

monorail

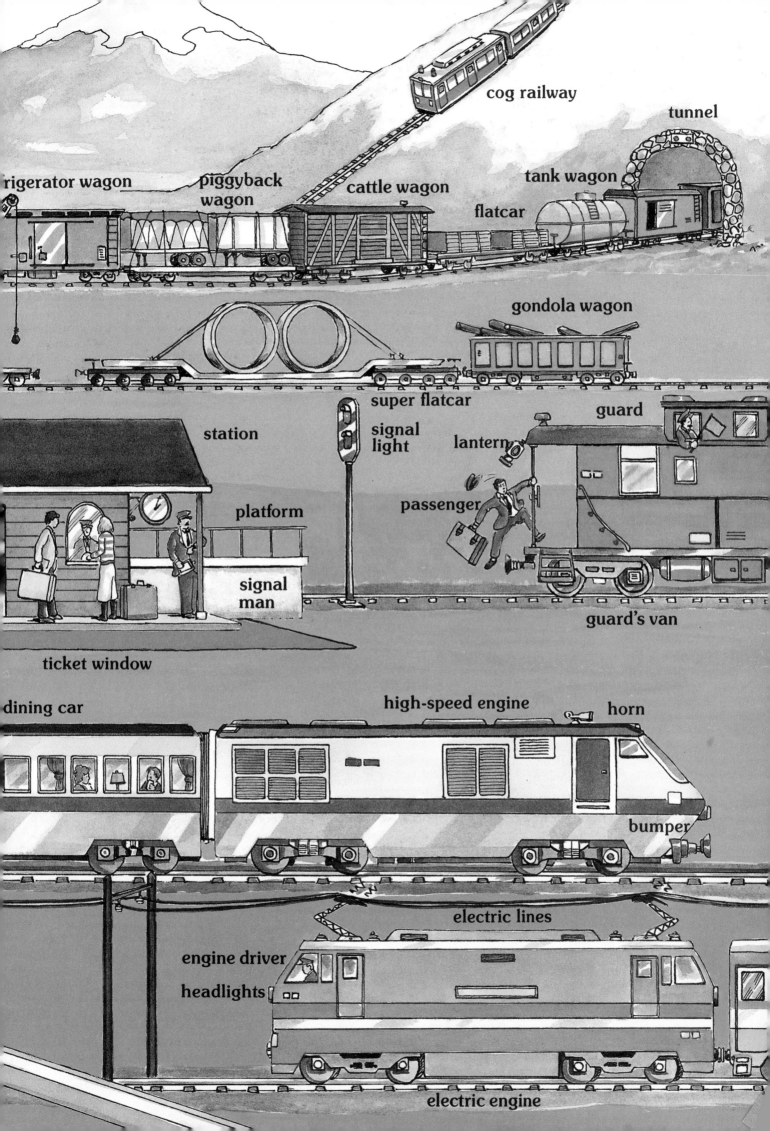

cog railway

tunnel

refrigerator wagon

piggyback wagon

cattle wagon

tank wagon

flatcar

gondola wagon

super flatcar

station

signal light

lantern

guard

platform

passenger

signal man

guard's van

ticket window

dining car

high-speed engine

horn

bumper

electric lines

engine driver

headlights

electric engine

IN THE HARBOUR

lighthouse

funnels

container boat

life boats

cargo containers

ocean liner

bridge

ferry

hovercraft

bell buoy

speedboat

tugboat

barge

outboard motor

mast

motorboat

sport fishing boat

oars

cabin

rudder

rowing boat

buoy

sloop

sailing boat

bow

stern

oil tanker

anchor

periscope

crow's nest

sails

submarine

rigging

ightship

bowsprit

clipper

trawler

hing nets

loading crane

pulley

freighter

flag

flagpole

deck

shipping crates

freight hatches

dock workers

sherman

grain sacks

rope

dock

freight lorry

mooring

raft

paddle

canoe

AT A BUILDING SITE

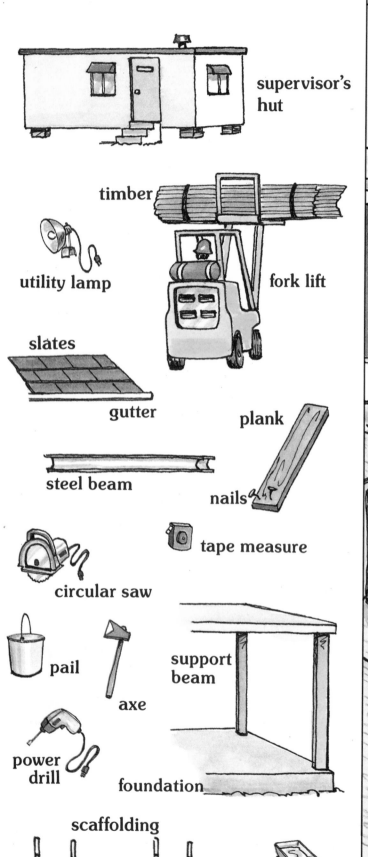

supervisor's hut

timber

utility lamp

fork lift

slates

gutter

plank

steel beam

nails

tape measure

circular saw

pail

support beam

axe

power drill

foundation

scaffolding

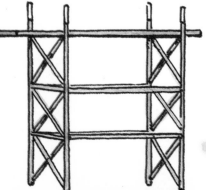

cement trough

pipe

cement mixer

handsaw

mitre box

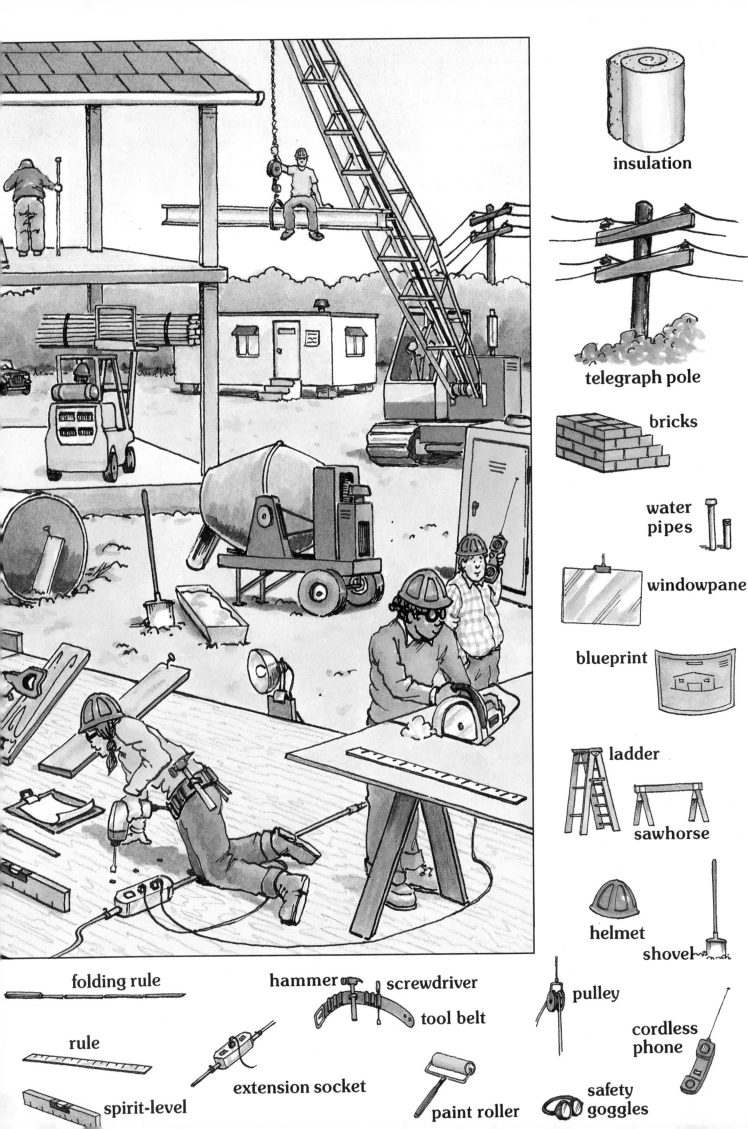

insulation

telegraph pole

bricks

water pipes

windowpane

blueprint

ladder

sawhorse

helmet

shovel

folding rule

hammer

screwdriver

tool belt

pulley

cordless phone

rule

extension socket

spirit-level

paint roller

safety goggles

IN THE OFFICE

desk

typewriter

radio

pie chart

chair

briefcase

paper cup holder

triangle

T-square

stool

skyline

adding machine

notice board

calculator

bookshelf

telephone

keyboard

earphones

dictating machine

computer terminal

printer

microphone

bar chart

slide projector

art supplies

envelope

clock

slides

stapler

desk tidy

tape

calendar

tape holder

photocopier

parcel

fire alarm

water cooler

postal scales

lamp

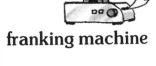
'in' tray

'out' tray

franking machine
letter

filing cabinet

pigeon holes

drawing board

paper clip

paper

ON THE ROAD

removal van

bus

bucket loader

dump lorry

construction
worker

shovels

tanker

detour sig

steam roller

bulldozer

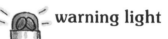
warning light

roadblock

car

van

water pump

digger

hydraulic
platform

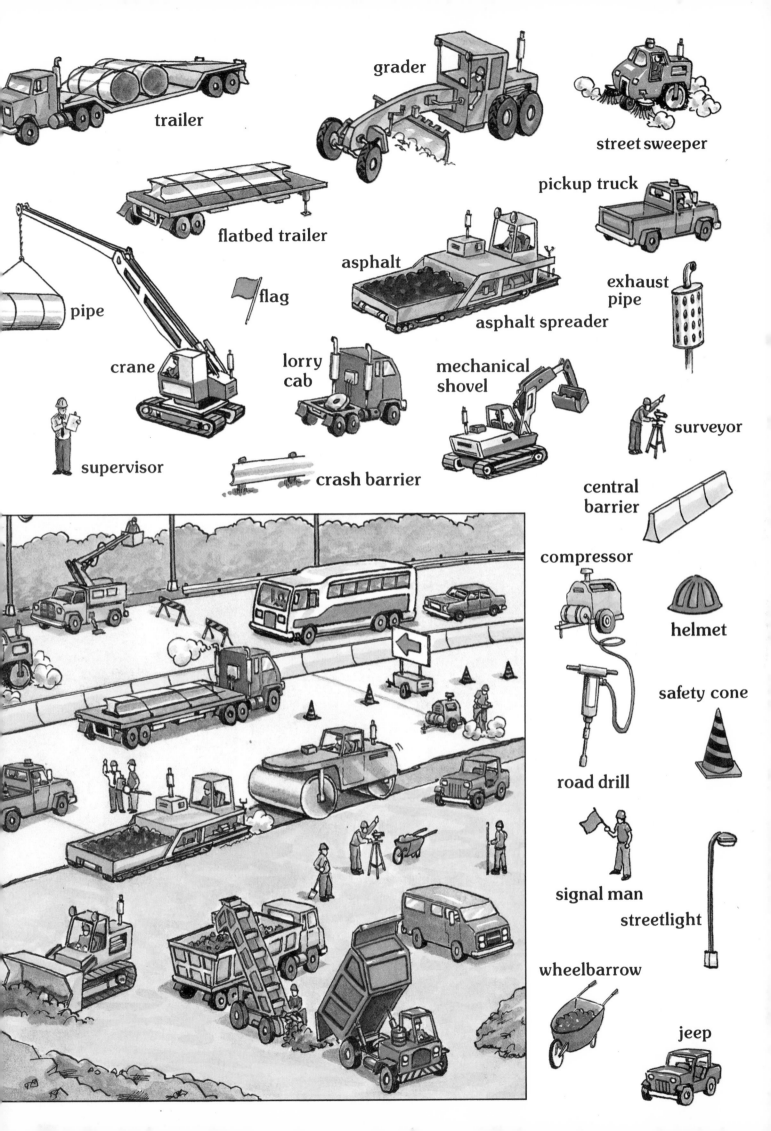

trailer

grader

street sweeper

pickup truck

flatbed trailer

asphalt

asphalt spreader

exhaust pipe

flag

pipe

crane

lorry cab

mechanical shovel

surveyor

supervisor

crash barrier

central barrier

compressor

helmet

safety cone

road drill

signal man

streetlight

wheelbarrow

jeep

WORLD AT WORK

A
adding machine
air filter
air hose
air pump
air traffic controller
ambulance
anchor
apron
art supplies
asphalt
asphalt spreader
awl
axe

B
bar chart
barge
battery
bell buoy
bicycle helmet
binoculars
blimp
blueprint
boarding ramp
bonnet
bookshelf
bow
bowsprit
bricks
bridge
briefcase
bucket loader
building bricks
bulldozer
bumper
buoy
bus

C
cabin
calculator
calendar
canoe

car
cargo containers
cargo plane
cart
cattle wagon
cement mixer
cement trough
central barrier
chair
circular saw
clipboard
clipper
clipper ship
clock
coal wagon
cockpit
coffee machine
cog railway
compressor
computer terminal
construction worker
container boat
control tower
convertible
conveyor belt
cordless phone
covered hopper
cowcatcher
crane wagon
crash barrier
crowbar
crow's nest

D
deck
desk
desk tidy
detour sign
dictating machine
diesel engine
digger
dining car

dock
docking director
docking tractor
dock workers
doll's house
dolly
double-door wagon
drawing board
dump lorry
dust bin

E
earphones
electric lines
electric engine
engine
engine driver
envelope
exhaust
exit sign
extension lead
extension socket

F
fan
fan belts
ferry
filing cabinet
fire alarm
fire engine
fisherman
fishing nets
flag
flagpole
flaps
flatbed trailer
flatcar
flight attendant
fluorescent light
folding rule
football
foundation
franking machine

WORD LIST

freighter
freight hatches
freight lorry
fridge
funnels
fuel tanker

G generator
gondola wagon
gooseneck trailer
grader
grain sacks
grease gun
guard
guard's van
gutter

H hammer
handsaw
hangars
headlamp
headlight
headlights
helicopter
helmet
high-speed engine
hopper
horn
hot air balloon
hubcap
hydraulic lift
hydraulic platform

I "in" tray
insulation

J jack
jack-in-the-box
jeep
jet engine
jetliner

jet walkway
jumbo jet

K keyboard

L ladder
lamp
landing gear
landing pad
lantern
letter
lifeboats
lighthouse
lightship
loader
loading crane
lorry cab
luggage
luggage trolley
lunch box

M mailbags
mast
mechanical shovel
microphone
mitre box
monorail
mooring
motorboat
motorcycle
motor oil cans

N nails
nose
notice board

O oars
observation carriage
ocean liner
oil spout
oil tanker

outboard motor
"out" tray

P packing material
paddle
pail
paint roller
paper
paper clip
paper cup holder
paper towel dispenser
parcel
passenger
passenger carriages
periscope
petrol cap
petrol pump
photocopier
pick-up truck
pie chart
pigeon holes
piggyback wagon
pipe
plane
plank
platform
pliers
polystyrene cups
porter
postal scales
power drill
pressure gauge
printer
private jet
propeller
propeller plane
public telephone
pulley

R radar dish
radiator

radio
raft
refrigerator wagon
removal van
rigging
road drill
roadblock marker
robot
rocking horse
roofrack
rope
rotors
rowing boat
rudder
rule
runway

S safety cone
safety goggles
safety helmet
sailing boat
sails
sawhorse
scaffolding
scissors
scissors loader
screwdriver
service lift
service station
   attendant
sewing machine
shipping crates
shovels
shunter
shuttle bus
signal light
signal man
skyline
slates
slide projector
slides

sloop
smokestack
spanner
speedboat
spirit level
sport fishing boat
sports car
spray gun
sprinkler
squeegee
stapler
station
station sign
steam engine
steam roller
steam whistle
steel beam
stern
stool
streetlight
street sweeper
submarine
super flatcar
supervisor
supervisor's hut
support beam
surveyor

T tail
tank wagon
tanker
tap
tape
tape holder
tape measure
taxicab
teddy bear
telegraph pole
telephone
ten speed bicycle
terminal

thread
ticket window
till
timber
timecards
time clock
toilet
tool belt
torch
toy duck
toy lorry
trawler
triangle
trolley
T-square
tugboat
tunnel
typewriter
tyre
tyre changer

U utility lamp

V vacuum cleaner
van
vending machine

W warning light
water bottle
water cooler
water pipes
water pump
welder
wheelbarrow
wheels
windowpane
windscreen wipers
wind sock
wing